Published by Vizye Publications, Shaynen Series in 2016
First edition; First printing

Design and writing © 2016 Bonni Goldberg
Cover design by Jessica Martin

ISBN 978-0-9967524-0-4

_____

(Your Name)

Jewish Holiday Journal

_____

(Year)

Welcome to Your Jewish Holiday Journal!

A Journal is…

- A great place to keep memories and ideas.
- Private or to share--you decide!

You can…

- Write, draw, doodle, paint, stick
- Color the Holiday titles and pictures
- Fill in this journal by yourself or get help
- Do the Word Scrambles, skip them, or challenge family and friends to unscramble (the answers are in the back of the journal).

This journal is for you to collect your ideas, memories, and feelings about the Jewish holidays for one year. Next year, you can start a new journal if you want to do it again.

Have fun! ☺

ROSH HASHANAH

Date_____

Word Scramble

weste _____

ewn _____

eray _____

This is the Jewish holiday to celebrate:

_____

The Story/Traditions of Rosh Hashanah:

_____

_____

_____

_____

_____

_____

_____

Draw, Doodle or Stick here:

This Rosh Hashanah
I hope/pray for:

Me

_____

_____

My family

_____

_____

Others

_____

_____

The World

_____

_____

Draw, Doodle or Stick here:

This year, this is how we celebrated Rosh Hashanah:

_____

_____

_____

_____

_____

_____

_____

Draw, Doodle or Stick here:

The best thing about
Rosh Hashanah is:

Draw, Doodle or Stick here:

_____

_____

_____

_____

The worst thing about
Rosh Hashanah is:

_____

_____

_____

_____

This year, I'm excited for:

_____

_____

_____

_____

YOM KIPPUR

Date_____

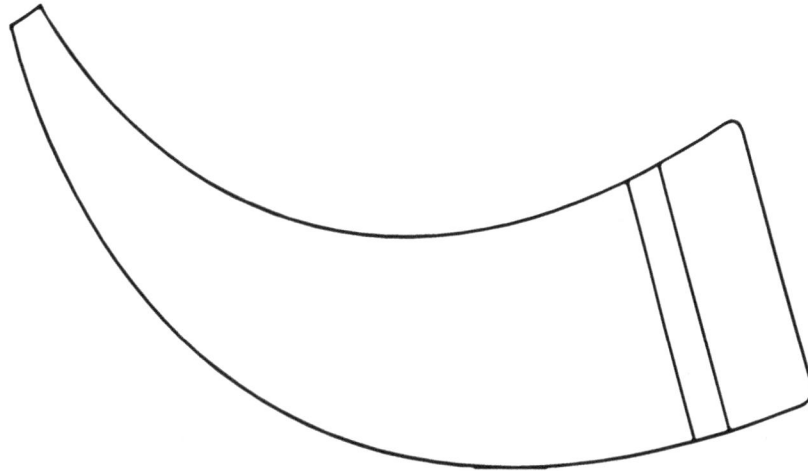

Word Scramble

rosry   _____

fsohra   _____

ryt   _____

This is the Jewish holiday to celebrate:

_____

The Story/Traditions of Yom Kippur:

_____

_____

_____

_____

_____

_____

_____

Draw, Doodle or Stick here:

This Yom Kippur
I hope/pray for:

Me

Draw, Doodle or Stick here:

_____

_____

My family

_____

_____

Others

_____

_____

The World

_____

_____

This year, this is how we celebrated Yom Kippur:

_____

_____

_____

_____

_____

_____

_____

Draw, Doodle or Stick here.

The best thing about
Yom Kippur is:

Draw, Doodle or Stick here:

_____

_____

_____

_____

The worst thing about
Yom Kippur is:

_____

_____

_____

_____

This year, I'm sorry about:

_____

_____

_____

_____

SUKKOT

Date_____

Word Scramble

kaksu   _____
tenuar   _____
syk   _____

This is the Jewish holiday to celebrate:

_____

The Story/Traditions of Sukkot:

_____

_____

_____

_____

_____

_____

_____

Draw, Doodle or Stick here:

This Sukkot
I hope/pray for:

Me

Draw, Doodle or Stick here:

_____

_____

My family

_____

_____

Others

_____

_____

The World

_____

_____

This year, this is how we celebrated Sukkot:

_____

_____

_____

_____

_____

_____

_____

Draw, Doodle or Stick here:

The best thing about
Sukkot is:

Draw, Doodle or Stick here:

_____

_____

_____

_____

The worst thing about
Sukkot is:

_____

_____

_____

_____

This year, I'm grateful for:

_____

_____

_____

_____

SIMCHAT TORAH

Date_____

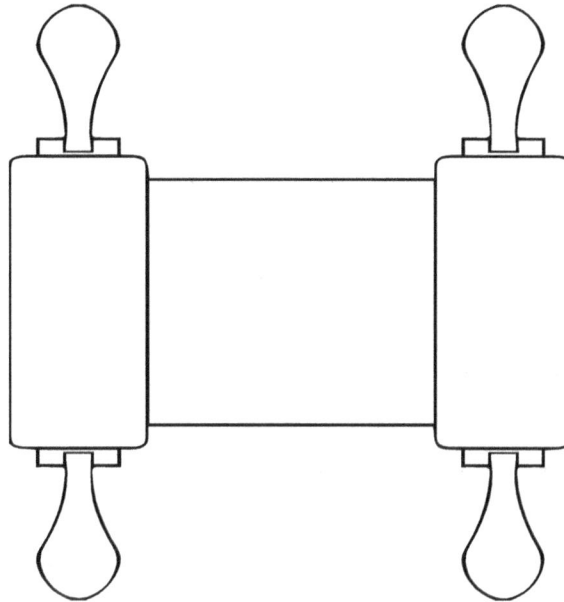

Word Scramble

horta   _____

wne   _____

oyj   _____

This is the Jewish holiday to celebrate:

_____

The Story/Traditions of Simchat Torah:

_____

_____

_____

_____

_____

_____

_____

Draw, Doodle or Stick here:

This Simchat Torah
I hope/pray for:

Me

Draw, Doodle or Stick here:

_____

_____

My family

_____

_____

Others

_____

_____

The World

_____

_____

This year, this is how we celebrated Simchat Torah:

_____

_____

_____

_____

_____

_____

_____

Draw, Doodle or Stick here:

The best thing about
Simchat Torah is:

Draw, Doodle or Stick here:

_____

_____

_____

_____

The worst thing about
Simchat Torah is:

_____

_____

_____

_____

I'm glad to start:

_____

_____

_____

_____

HANUKKAH

Date_____

Word Scramble

romaneh _____
hlgti _____
iclirame _____

This is the Jewish holiday to celebrate:

_____

The Story/Traditions of Hannukah:

_____

_____

_____

_____

_____

_____

_____

Draw, Doodle or Stick here:

This Hannukah
I hope/pray for:

Me

Draw, Doodle or Stick here:

_____

_____

My family

_____

_____

Others

_____

_____

The World

_____

_____

This year, this is how we celebrated Hannukah:

_____

_____

_____

_____

_____

_____

_____

Draw, Doodle or Stick here:

The best thing about
Hannukah is:

Draw, Doodle or Stick here:

_____

_____

_____

_____

The worst thing about
Hannukah is:

_____

_____

_____

_____

The miracle I would like:

_____

_____

_____

_____

TU B'SHEVAT

Date_____

Word Scramble

serte   _____
idbryhatd   _____
elvo   _____

This is the Jewish holiday to celebrate:

_____

The Story/Traditions of Tu B'Shevat:

_____

_____

_____

_____

_____

_____

_____

Draw, Doodle or Stick here:

This Tu B'Shevat
I hope/pray for:

Me

Draw, Doodle or Stick here:

_____

_____

My family

_____

_____

Others

_____

_____

The World

_____

_____

This year, this is how we celebrated Tu B'Shevat:

_____

_____

_____

_____

_____

_____

_____

Draw, Doodle or Stick here:

The best thing about
Tu B'Shevat is:

Draw, Doodle or Stick here:

_____

_____

_____

_____

The worst thing about
Tu B'Shevat is:

_____

_____

_____

_____

What I love best in nature:

_____

_____

_____

_____

PURIM

Date_____

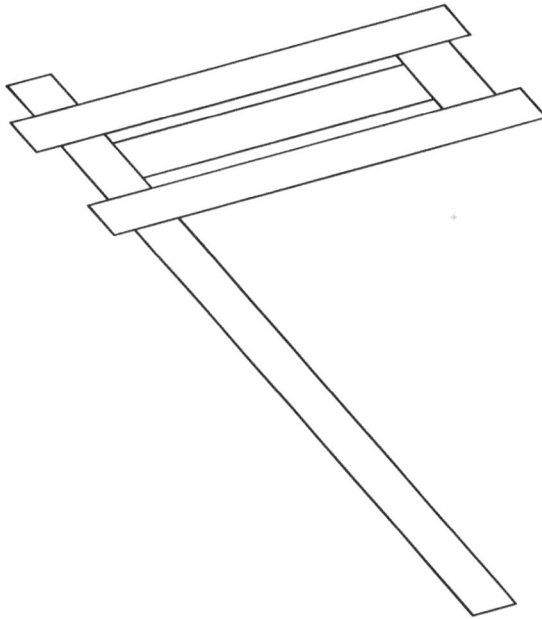

Word Scramble

serhte _____

mahna _____

ebvar _____

This is the Jewish holiday to celebrate:

_____

The Story/Traditions of Purim:

_____

_____

_____

_____

_____

_____

_____

Draw, Doodle or Stick here:

This Purim
I hope/pray for:

Me

_____

_____

My family

_____

_____

Others

_____

_____

The World

_____

_____

Draw, Doodle or Stick here:

This year, this is how we celebrated Purim:

_____

_____

_____

_____

_____

_____

_____

Draw, Doodle or Stick here:

The best thing about
Purim is:

Draw, Doodle or Stick here:

_____

_____

_____

_____

The worst thing about
Purim is:

_____

_____

_____

_____

This year, I'm brave about:

_____

_____

_____

_____

PESACH (PASSOVER)

Date_____

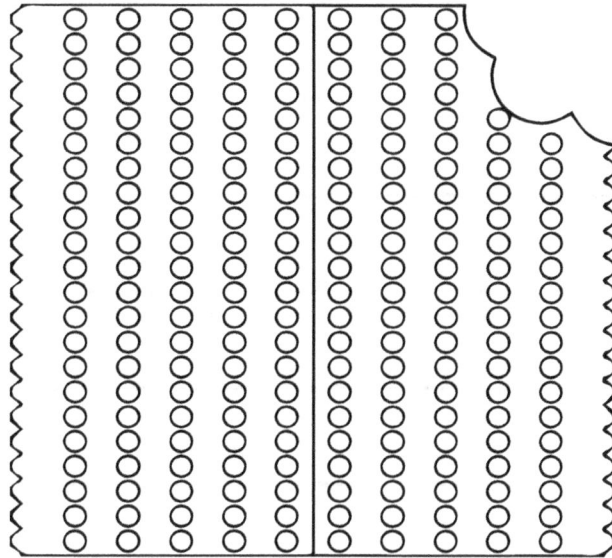

Word Scramble

zatam   _____

deser   _____

efer   _____

This is the Jewish holiday to celebrate:

_____

The Story/Traditions of Pesach (Passover):

_____

_____

_____

_____

_____

_____

_____

Draw, Doodle or Stick here:

This Pesach (Passover)
I hope/pray for:

Me

_____

_____

My family

_____

_____

Others

_____

_____

The World

_____

_____

Draw, Doodle or Stick here:

This year, this is how we celebrated Pesach (Passover):

_____

_____

_____

_____

_____

_____

_____

Draw, Doodle or Stick here:

The best thing about
Pesach (Passover) is:

Draw, Doodle or Stick here:

_____

_____

_____

_____

The worst thing about
Pesach (Passover) is:

_____

_____

_____

_____

I'm glad I'm free so I can:

_____

_____

_____

_____

YOM HA'ATZMA'UT

Date_____

Word Scramble

rilesa   _____
meho   _____
nald   _____

This is the Jewish holiday to celebrate:

_____

The Story/Traditions of
Yom Ha'atzma'ut:

_____

_____

_____

_____

_____

_____

Draw, Doodle or Stick here:

This Yom Ha'atzma'ut
I hope/pray for:

Me

_____

_____

My family

_____

_____

Others

_____

_____

The World

_____

_____

Draw, Doodle or Stick here:

This year, this is how we celebrated Yom Ha'atzma'ut:

_____

_____

_____

_____

_____

_____

_____

Draw, Doodle or Stick here:

The best thing about
Yom Ha'atzma'ut is:

Draw, Doodle or Stick here:

_____

_____

_____

_____

The worst thing about
Yom Ha'atzma'ut is:

_____

_____

_____

_____

To me, Israel is:

_____

_____

_____

_____

SHAVUOT

Date_____

אבגדה
וזחטי

Word Scramble

wjes   _____
artho   _____
yimafl _____

This is the Jewish holiday to celebrate:

_____

The Story/Traditions of Shavuot:

_____

_____

_____

_____

_____

_____

_____

Draw, Doodle or Stick here:

This Shavuot
I hope/pray for:

Me

_____

_____

My family

_____

_____

Others

_____

_____

The World

_____

_____

Draw, Doodle or Stick here:

This year, this is how we celebrated Shavuot:

_____

_____

_____

_____

_____

_____

_____

Draw, Doodle or Stick here:

The best thing about
Shavuot is:

Draw, Doodle or Stick here:

_____

_____

_____

_____

The worst thing about
Shavuot is:

_____

_____

_____

_____

To me, being Jewish means:

_____

_____

_____

_____

Word Scramble Answers

Rosh Hashanah
sweet
new
year

Yom Kippur
sorry
shofar
try

Sukkot
sukka
nature
stars

Simchat Torah
Torah
new
joy

Hannukah
menorah
light
miracle

Tu B'Shevat
trees
birthday
love

Purim
Esther
Haman
brave

Passover
matzah
seder
free

Yom Ha'atzma'ut
Israel
home
land

Shavuot
Jews
Torah
family

www.ingramcontent.com/pod-product-compliance
Lightning Source LLC
Chambersburg PA
CBHW080401030426
42334CB00024B/2957